Fantastic Fishing Funnies

Skyhorse Publishing books may be purchased in bulk at special discounts for sales promotion, corporate gifts, fund-raising, or educational purposes. Special editions can also be created to specifications. For details, contact the Special Sales Department, Skyhorse Publishing, 307 West 36th Street, 11th Floor, New York, NY 10018 or info@skyhorsepublishing.com.

Skyhorse® and Skyhorse Publishing® are registered trademarks of Skyhorse Publishing, Inc.®, a Delaware corporation.

Visit our website at www.skyhorsepublishing.com.

10 9 8 7 6 5 4 3 2 1

Library of Congress Cataloging-in-Publication Data is available on file.

ISBN: 978-1-62873-684-7

Printed in China

Fantastic Fishing Funnies

JONNY HAWKINS

Skyhorse Publishing

"Before I continue this conversation, I *am* speaking to your face, right?"

"I wasn't feeling so well, so I came to the dock."

Levels of Heaven

"Do you see the one that took your bait?"

"Looks like we're going to get a shower."

"I need a GPS to find my tackle box!"

"It's a good day for panfish."

"'Cuz when I go fishing on our anniversary, all I catch is flak."

"I don't know. I only mentioned it
once on Fishbook!"

"Haven't had any action all day. I
get a feeling we're going to have one
epic bite soon."

"I went ice fishing and all I caught was a cold."

"So far, I've caught two of everything."

"He'll do anything to keep other fishermen away from his spot."

"Let's get out of here! Old Butterfingers himself will be coming down next."

"Keep an eye out, Marge. I hear there are real hogs in this lake."

"Don't worry, Alice, I'll never leave you."

"Nice visiting with you. I'll catch you on the fly."

"Throw me the rod!"

"A heartwarming novel, I'm sure."

"Caterpillars leave me feeling so worm and fuzzy."

"She overturned it."

"Haven't you ever seen Cellfish
before?"

"You buy the boat and I get a free vacation."

"I suppose the same old fish story,
'You should have seen the one that
got away!'"

"Eat plenty of mercury and they'll leave you alone."

"It's really creeping me out. No matter where I go in the bowl, his eyes follow me."

"What SPF is your sunscreen?"

Frank couldn't get a hole-in-one in
golf, but he got one fishing.

Used Carp Salesman

"Now, that's a moray!"

"When you advertised a big fly sale,
I thought …"

"I distinctly ordered anchovies!"

"I'm short on coins. Can I give you your change back in crickets?"

"This looks like a good spot."

"I told you not to touch that handle!"

"Little bit of a bend ... but, hey ... nice action."

"Honey, could you reconsider your vow to never trim your beard until you catch a muskie?"

Fishing for sheepshead

"Better throw it back. The attention
you'd give it would put a serious strain on
our relationship."

"Great! I heard the camera adds
10 pounds!"

"I don't think I would have the patience to wait that long for a bite."

"You really should try catching one, Herb. It would do wonders for all that hostility!"

"He's an exchange student from
another school."

"Really? You outsmarted him?! I didn't know that was possible."

Ed is a fisherman who never lies.
He tells all his stories sitting up.

"Why do they stink like fish when they've been bathing this whole time?!"

"I threw it back because it was too big.
I'm on a diet, remember?"

"I'm so proud of this—you'd never know
it's just wallpaper."

"Stickbait, of course."

"You know how I throw everything back? Turns out, I accidentally threw back your Winston."

String Quartet

"No, but I caught some good vibes."

Worm ranching

"I'll go get help if you can hang on the line."

Self-cleaning fish

"I'm giving my fish mosquito barbecue."

"Heckuva bird's nest, Morris."

"Uh oh—the devil's triangle."

"Our boat is the latest in stealth technology."

"He'd swim the widest river for me, but only if there were fish there."

"Worst case of backlash I've ever seen!"

"Look! I caught a fish!"

**Claude finds he can catch more fish using
barb wire.**

"You have trout fever."

"Calvin always did find the most far-out fishing spot."

Worm pranks

"Sure, I smoked salmon—but I never inhaled."

Albert goes in for an angler-o-plasty.

"Cool. We'll use it for bait."

"Might I suggest the veal?"

"I come from a long line of fishermen."

"**Anything bitin'?**"

"Quick—let's put it away. Here comes the game warden!"

**"Quick, give me that classic photo
pose ... perfect."**

"Care for a wake-up call of the wild?"

"As a webmaster, I'm all about fly fishing online."

"Something tells me this is a real hot spot."

"How can you eat at a time like
this?!!"

"Heyyy ... nice bass boat, Stan!"

"You've got snail mail."

"Go get a camera ... and a marriage counselor."

"Oh, lighten up, Maude—it's just a
silly old broom."

"Lets just say we caught hundreds of keepers and kept them in their natural habitat."

**Edith's means of gaining leverage was
a minor annoyance to Howard.**

"Check it out, Dad! I parked it perfectly!"

"I didn't land any trout, but I feel
good about taking my pet fly out for a
swim.

**The last of civilization to give in to a
cordless society.**

"That's not what I meant by 'bottom bumping with jigs'."

"I think you may appreciate the bite I just got, Durwood."

Unmitigated gull

"Man, the humidity sure is high today."

"I'm only interested in fillets."

"Bottom hugger, I s'pect."

"I threw back a throwback and threw out my back."

"This one needs to be cleaned."

"You don't catch crappie that way."

Homer decided against smoking fish.

"I don't know about you, but Irwin's new
trophy wife kinda gives me the creeps."

"I'm afraid your markings make you a
most desirable catch."

"That kind of junk food can get you hooked."

"You struggle and fight and finally catch me and then
you just let me go?!
What—are you afraid of commitment or something?!"

"I love you to the core."

"I refuse to eat anything that eats leeches."

Vince would do just about anything to catch a fish, but this time, Helen thought, he went overboard.

"You'll never catch sheepshead with a wolf spider."

"I gave up smoking and took up
fishing."

"Dad—I'm really getting caught up in this awesome scenery! ... Dad? ... Dad?!"

"It combines my two favorite sports."

"Rotate your tire!"

"No, Billy, that's not how you side cast."

"That new bungee fishing line was a
mistake."

"The first thing you need to do is toss your chum overboard."

"I think I see why you have water on the knee."

Overcrowding at Lake Pontchartrain led to the advent of bunk boats.

Row Rage

"Oh sure, you want to feed me—but there are always strings attached!"

"That's the best fisherman I've ever seen. He just caught a fish in a mirage."

"Topwater bait."

"Yeah, I hear ya. Sometimes those buggers swallow the whole shmeer."

"It's to help find certain saltwater fish ... you know, a herring aid."

Where bearded men store bait

The bookie, the rookie, and the brookie

"Even when I'm fishing, the only thing I
catch is flounder."

The great walleye of China

"I'm an IRS agent ... I catch everything."

"Must be allergies … my nose is plugged."

"Did you mistakenly bring your toolbox again, dear?"

"I hate to eat ya, 'cuz you seem so down
to earth, worm."

"Ahhh," Horace thought, "spring is in the air."

When a bride should recognize that there's trouble

Chemistry glassblower Roy Wentz drags a tube.

"It's just that I've never met a Dolly Parton trout before."

Betty Croaker

"You're using WHAT kind of bug for bait!?"

When boots fight back

When plumbers fish

How reel men line dance

"Heyyy! ... you were supposed to build a *deck*, not a *dock*!!"

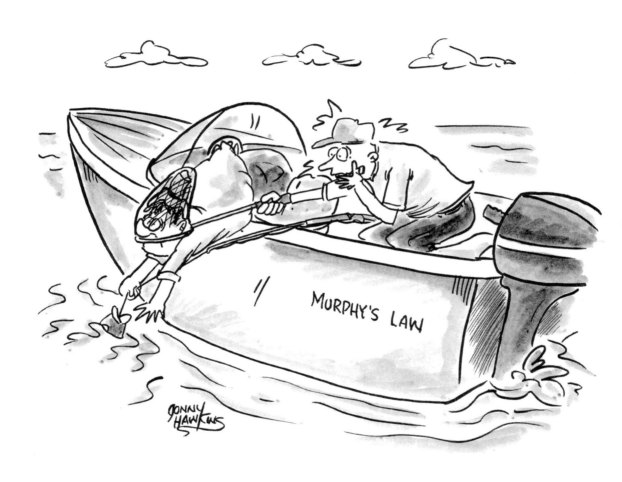

Jeremy's first-time fishing jitters are apparent.

"How much do you put in to clean one of
these suckers?"

"Let's open this baby up a notch and see
what it can *really* do."

Horse fly fishing

"A towering fortress against the teeming shores safely guiding ships in with its radiant light? Nah, it's a bait shop."

**Bill's wife bakes him an authentic
longjohnboat.**